Before using these books...

☞ A teacher/counselor manual is separately available for guiding students in the use of these workbooks.

✍ To prevent bleed-through, it is recommended that water-based, rather than spirit-based, markers or pens be used in this workbook.

Important

This book is not intended as a treatment tool or to be utilized for diagnostic or investigative purposes. It is not designed for and should not be recommended or suggested for use in any unsupervised, self-help or self-therapy setting, group or situation. Professionals who use this book are exercising their own professional judgement and take full responsibility for doing so.

The STARS LifeSkills Program

Teacher/Counselor Manual

Learning About Anger

Learning More About Anger

Knowing Yourself

Getting Along with Others

Respecting Others

How Drugs and Alcohol Affect Us

Learning More About Anger

Jan Stewart

Illustrated by Cecilia Bowman

ISBN 1-63026-806-2

© 2003 Jan Stewart and Hunter House

Design and layout Jinni Fontana © 2003 Hunter House

First U.S. edition published in 2003 by Hunter House.

For further information, contact Hunter House, Inc.

STARS: Steps to Achieving Real-life Skills

Learning More About Anger

Dear Student:

This workbook is part of a program to help you learn some real-life skills. You may already have some of these skills, and the information may just be a reminder or a review. If the information is new to you, then it is possible for you to learn skills and strategies that can help you for the rest of your life.

If you are unable to complete any section, leave it blank and come back to it later. If you are still unsure, ask your parent or guardian to assist you. If this is not possible, ask the person who gave you the workbook. On the next page is a glossary of words that are used in the workbook. Read this before you begin.

Please remember to have your parent or guardian fill out the last page.

Thank you for your cooperation.

Name of Student: _____

Adviser: _____

Assignment Date: _____

Completion Date: _____

Glossary

Antecedent — something that happens before something else

Anxious — feeling tense or nervous

Behavior — the way someone acts

Belittled — made to feel small or unworthy

Consequence — the result of your behavior

Humiliated — shamed or disrespected by others

Insecure — lacking confidence

Provoke — irritate or push someone

Relaxation Technique — a skill or activity you can use to calm yourself

Response — a reaction or answer using actions or words

Self-talk — words or phrases you say to yourself

Technique — a method or way of doing something

Tension — a feeling of stress, strain, or anxiety

Triggers — situations, events or behavior that provoke or activate your anger

Learning More About Anger

In *Learning About Anger,* you had a chance to learn about several topics related to anger. Here is a quick outline of the major topics in the first workbook:

1. Emotions related to anger

2. Anger triggers

3. Knowing your anger levels

4. Assertive, aggressive, and passive expression

5. Relaxation techniques

6. Self-talk

7. Assertion techniques

This unit will go into more depth on these topics and will also include some new information on assessing anger and problem solving. You may wish to use your first workbook to help you work through this one.

1. What is anger?

   _____

   _____

   _____

   _____

2. What are four emotions that may be inside a person who is showing that he or she is angry?

   1. _____

   2. _____

   _____

   _____

3. What are your anger triggers?

   _____

   _____

   _____

   _____

   _____

   _____

4. Define the following words and give an example of what each personality type would do.

Aggressive: _____

_____

_____

Example:_____

_____

_____

Assertive:_____

_____

_____

Example:_____

_____

_____

Passive: _____

_____

_____

Example:_____

_____

_____

5. Which response to anger is most likely to get you what you wanted, without having a negative consequence?

       ☐ Aggressive

       ☐ Assertive

       ☐ Passive

Explain: _____

_____

_____

_____

_____

6. What are two things you could say to make yourself calm down?

1._____

2._____

7. How do each of the following assertion techniques work? Use your own words.

The Skipping CD

_____

_____

_____

Friendly Reflection

_____

_____

_____

The Elevator

_____

_____

_____

Short Circuit

_____

_____

_____

"I" Messages

_____

_____

_____

Ignore

_____

_____

_____

The Emotion Roller Coaster

Using the "Emotion Roller Coaster" picture on page 9, **write down the emotion** that you think best describes how the person is feeling in each situation.

1. Tia was walking through the school hall and she passed a group of boys from her grade. When she walked by she heard one of the boys say, "Look at the big loser, Tia."

How might Tia have felt? _____

_____

_____

2. Carlos was playing defense for his hockey team. Carlos accidentally let the puck go by, and the other team scored. Carlos' dad yelled, "What's wrong with you, can't you do anything right?"

How might Carlos have felt? _____

_____

_____

3. Gabriella is about to take a final exam in math, her worst subject.

What might Gabriella be feeling? _____

_____

_____

4. Simone comes home from school and finds out her dog has been hit by a car.

What might Simone be feeling? _____

_____

_____

Illustration by Rita D. Procyshyn. Used with permission.

5. Josette and Roberto are going out for the first time to a movie. They both like each other very much.

    *How do you think Josette and Roberto might feel?*_____

    _____

    _____

6. Antonio is trying to print his twenty-page report on cars with his home computer. His report is due tomorrow morning and his printer keeps jamming.

    How do you think Antonio is feeling? _____

    _____

    _____

7. Monique and Shalonda are working on a science project together. Every time they plan to meet, Monique forgets to show up. Shalonda has done almost all the project on her own, and Monique is bragging about how much work she has done.

    *How might Shalonda feel?*_____

    _____

    _____

8. Chen, Jose, Matthew, and Carl are good friends. Chen, Carl, and Jose have all arranged to go out to play baseball at lunch. They don't want Matthew along, so they tell him that they aren't playing today. When Matthew goes out at lunch, he sees them playing.

    How might Matthew feel after he sees them? _____

    _____

    _____

9. Someone has broken into Marita's locker, stolen her wallet, and ripped up her textbooks and binders.

What might Marita be feeling? _____

_____

_____

10. Keith and Tamika are walking through the park at night. Without warning, a group of six people rush up behind them and start demanding that they give them money.

How might Tamika and Keith feel? _____

_____

_____

Pick two more emotions from the roller coaster and write two of your own situations below.

Situation: _____

_____

Emotion:_____

Situation: _____

_____

Emotion:_____

There are many more emotions people feel besides the ones on the roller coaster. **Write down three more emotions that have not been mentioned.**

1._____

2._____

3._____

Remember:

It's possible to have different feelings about the same situation.

Facing Our Feelings

Match each face with an emotion from the list. Note that some of the faces may represent more than one emotion.

bored   lonely   disappointed   enraged   frightened   angry

embarrassed   happy   hopeful   excited   surprised   sad

mad   uncertain   confused   scared

1. _____   2. _____   3. _____

4. _____   5. _____   6. _____

7. _____   8. _____   9. _____

What Are Your Anger Warning Signs?

We usually have warning signs before we "blast off" into anger. What tends to get you angry? What are some things you say to yourself when you get angry? How does your body react to anger?

List some things that might make you feel angry.

_____

_____

_____

When you are angry, what do you usually do? _____

_____

_____

How does what you do help you? _____

_____

_____

_____

How does what you do not help you? _____

_____

_____

_____

Fill in the chart on the next page with some of your personal reactions to anger.

Triggers
(What occurs that results in anger?)
e.g., insults, frustration, worrying

_____

_____

_____

_____

_____

Mental Warning Signs
(What are you saying inside?)
e.g., "Now I feel totally awful."

_____

_____

_____

_____

_____

Physical Signs & Triggers
(How is your body reacting?)
e.g., sweating, red face, clenched fists

_____

_____

_____

_____

Illustration by Rita D. Procyshyn. Used with permission.

Responses to Anger

There are three ways that people generally express their anger: aggressively, passively, and assertively.

Aggressive anger:	Involves demanding your rights without thinking about the rights of others. This type of anger hurts people either emotionally, physically, or psychologically.
Aggressive people . . .	Blame others. Use physical or verbal violence. Bully or push people around. Yell or scream at others.
Passive anger:	Involves keeping your anger inside, and not dealing with the issue. This anger could result in feeling like you want to get even. Examples of passive anger include not talking to the other person, spreading rumors, and damaging people's property.
Passive people . . .	Make excuses. Don't want to express themselves. Blame themselves.
Assertive anger:	Involves standing up for your own rights and, at the same time, respecting the rights of others. This type of anger is expressed directly and in a non-threatening way to the other person involved.
Assertive people . . .	Use a variety of techniques to respond to anger. Express their feelings and thoughts to others. Are honest with themselves and others

Assertive people have the best results!

What Would They Do?

1. You're supposed to go to the mall after school with your friend, Chris. He tells you at lunch that he has invited Kareem to come along. You don't like Kareem because he is a bully and always has to be the center of attention.

What would a passive person do? _____

_____

What would an aggressive person do? _____

_____

What would an assertive person do? _____

_____

2. You go into a restaurant with your friend and take a booth in a section near other customers. The servers walk past, serve the other tables, and then they disappear. It's getting late and you need to get home soon.

What would a passive person do? _____

_____

What would an aggressive person do? _____

_____

What would an assertive person do? _____

_____

3. Your grandmother, who has always been prejudiced, is unhappy that some of your friends are of a different race. When you visit her, she tells you that she disapproves.

What would a passive person do? _____

_____

What would an aggressive person do? _____

_____

What would an assertive person do? _____

_____

4. You are riding your bike on a busy street and a car cuts you off. Both of you then come up to the same stoplight, and the driver rolls down the window and tells you to go ride on a street that doesn't have as much traffic.

What would a passive person do? _____

_____

What would an aggressive person do? _____

_____

What would an assertive person do? _____

_____

Instead of Blowing Up...

Let off some steam and keep yourself cool

If you keep your angry feelings bottled up, sooner or later you will blow up. When we blow up, we tend to do things that we later regret. There are many ways to let off steam before that happens. Some people like to be physically active while others like to think things over. Some people like to be around other people while others prefer to be alone. **Add a few of your own ideas to the picture below.**

Go for a walk

Take deep breaths

Talk to the person

Cool off, don't blow up!

Counting Backwards & Imagining a Calm Place

Counting backwards from twenty is a technique you can use to relax yourself. Start at twenty and then slowly count backwards to zero. As you do this, imagine being in a calm and pleasant place. Think of a safe place you can remember, or a place you've never been. Put yourself in the picture while you count to calm yourself down.

20...19...18...17...

16...15...14...13...

12...11...10...9...

8...7...6...5...

4...3...2...1...

0

Ahhh...that's better.   STOP...COUNT...THINK

In the space below, draw a picture of yourself in your calm, relaxing place. Use your imagination—you can be anywhere you want. Even loud places can be calming for some people. There are no wrong answers. Add some color to show what it looks like in more detail.

Be Responsible for Your Actions

"We're all responsible for what we feel, but sometimes we let strong emotions like anger control us. If that happens, we act in ways that we might regret later, once we have a chance to think about it. The trick is to be in touch with our feelings all the time. In the case of a situation that might provoke an angry response, we need to learn to identify our triggers so that we prevent trouble ahead. This will help us think before we act."

Source: *Men for Change. Healthy Relationships Curriculum.* Halifax: Halifax County-Bedford District School Board, p. 21, 1994.

In many cases, people resort to violence when they are not in control. Violence may come in many forms such as:

- Physical abuse

- Sexual abuse

- Emotional or psychological abuse

Violence is an extreme way to control other people. Violence usually occurs because someone is mis-using his or her power over another person.

List as many words as you can that come to your mind when you hear the word VIOLENCE.

_____ _____

_____ _____

_____ _____

_____ _____

_____ _____

_____ _____

_____ _____

Listening to Others

You can learn a lot about an issue or topic by simply listening to what other people say. **Ask a parent, teacher, or community member the questions below to survey his or her opinions about violence in society.**

1. How closely have you experienced violence, in one form or another?

1	2	3	4	5	6	7	8	9	10
very close (personal experience)		people I know			stories I hear				no experience

2. Do you think violence in our society is getting worse? Why or why not?

_____

_____

_____

3. What do you believe can be done to decrease violence in society?

_____

_____

_____

_____

4. What does violence mean to you?

_____

_____

_____

_____

Name of person surveyed: _____

Self Assessment of Anger

Do you know your ABCs?

These are different ABCs that can help you assess your anger.

A stands for **antecedent**

B stands for **behavior**

C stands for **consequence**

The **behavior** is what you do in response to the antecedent—how you think and feel.

- How does your body react?

- Did you yell, punch, kick, cry?

- Did you say something you regret?

- Did you feel like getting even?

- What are your triggers?

- Were you in control?

An **antecedent** is something that happens before you get angry.

- Where are you?

- How do you feel?

- Are you hungry?

- Are you tired?

- Who is with you?

The **consequence** is the result of your behavior.

- Did you get hurt?

- Did you hurt someone else?

- Did you get in trouble?

- Did the situation get worse?

- Did the situation get better?

How to Use the ABCs

Reviewing the details of a negative situation helps to prevent it from happening again. **Write down what happens before, during, and after an incident.**

Here is an example:

A *I was walking around at the mall with my friend. A group of kids walked by and gave us a mean look.*

B *I got mad and yelled back at them.*

C *They all turned back, surrounded us, and beat us up. Now I have a black eye and a broken wrist.*

Pick a situation when you have been in trouble, either at home or at school. Use the sheet about ABCs to help you.

A _____
_____
_____

B _____
_____
_____

C _____
_____
_____

Situations can also end positively. Your response to an event will lead to either a positive or negative consequence. Here is an example of a situation that ended positively because of the way the person behaved or responded to the antecedent.

A *I was walking around at the mall with my friend. A group of kids walked by and gave us a mean look.*

B *I felt angry, but I walked away and didn't say anything*

C *The situation didn't get worse and no one was physically hurt.*

Sometimes the best response is no response—it's not worth it. Some people are looking for trouble and they want you to get mad—not getting hooked into their plan is being in control.

Try one on your own. This can be a real or imagined situation.

_____

_____

_____

_____

_____

_____

_____

_____

_____

Problem Identification

A problem identification sheet is a guide to help you fill out the specific details of an event. Being specific is important because it tells you how to avoid the situation in the future. Think about the last time you had a conflict or a problem. **Fill out the rest of this sheet to the best of your ability.**

Name: _____

Date: _____ ☐ Morning ☐ Afternoon ☐ Evening

What happened? _____

_____

_____

_____

Where were you? _____

What were you thinking? _____

_____

What did you do? Was there a positive or negative consequence?_____

_____

How did you handle yourself?

1	2	3	4	5
Poorly	Not so well	Okay	Good	Great

How angry were you?

1	2	3	4	5
Extremely angry	Really angry	Moderately angry	Mildly angry	Not at all angry

Did you feel any other emotion? If yes, what did you feel? _____

_____

_____

Problem Solving I

Gathering facts about how you usually solve problems can help you find ways to improve. **Answer the following question in the space provided.**

DO _____

SAY _____

FEEL _____

How do you usually solve a problem? _____

_____

_____

_____

When was the last time you had to make a tough decision or solve a particular problem?

_____

_____

_____

What happened? How did it turn out? _____

_____

_____

If the same situation happened again, what would you do? _____

_____

_____

_____

Problem Solving II

Problems are a fact of life. Picture yourself making a decision about where to go for the weekend when two different friends have invited you out. How would you make the decision about where to go? How do you decide on a topic to write about for English class? Learning how to work out your problems and making decisions are skills you can use for the rest of your life.

To help guide you through the process, remember the word **SOLVE.** This is what it stands for:

S   **State** the problem

O   **Outline** your options

L   **List** the good and bad points of the options you like

V   **Visualize** the outcome

E   **Execute** your plan and **evaluate** your results

State the problem. When you have a decision to make, state what the problem is and try to be as specific as possible. For example, suppose you were accused of stealing something in a store. You didn't steal anything, and you need to respond to the clerk without the situation getting out of control.

Outline your options. Decide what you can do about the situation. Brainstorm all the ideas you can think of. For example, in private you could approach the person accusing you and explain the situation; or you could call your parents to explain things to them. Think of all the ideas you can, and, if it's possible, write them down.

List the good and bad points of the options you like. Pick the options that you think are the best. Maybe some of your options could be changed or joined together into an even better idea. At this time you do not have to be worried about details.

Visualize the outcome. Go over some of your responses to the problem situation. Think to yourself: "What will happen if I…? Think ahead and try to picture what the result will be if you choose a particular option. "How will it affect what I feel, need, and want? How will it affect others? How will it relate to what I and my family believe?" Once you have thought about the outcome of using your options, pick the best one and decide what you will do.

Execute your plan and evaluate the results. The final step is to act out your plan and then see if you made a decision that helped you or not. Ask yourself, "Did things turn out the way I thought? Is the solution better than if I hadn't done anything? What are the consequences of this solution?" Remember, just like athletes need to practice their sport over and over again, you may need some practice to find the best solution to solve the problem. However, with a lot of practice, you can be a good problem solver!

Try using the SOLVE method to solve any of the following problems. **Choose one of the following problem situations and circle the number beside it.**

1. You notice your friend stealing something from a store, and he or she wants you to help get it outside without being caught.

2. You and your brother want to watch different shows at the same time, on the only TV you have.

3. A friend of yours wants you to lie to her parents so that she can stay out late with her boyfriend.

4. The teacher is making you work on the big science project with a boy who always bullies you.

5. A friend told you a secret, but you know that his or her safety could be in danger if you don't tell an adult.

After you have chosen one situation, follow the SOLVE steps to work through the problem. You may need to use your imagination to decide on the entire situation.

S (STATE the dilemma) _____

_____

O (OUTLINE your options) _____

_____

L (LIST the good and bad points of the options you like)_____

_____

V (VISUALIZE the outcome)_____

_____

E (EXECUTE your plan and EVALUATE the results) _____

Which part was the most difficult to do? _____

Explain why it was difficult. _____

_____

Journal Writing—Reflecting

Take a moment to think about the work you have done in this workbook. **Jot down some words about how you felt working on this workbook.** From there, use a sentence starter to write about what you have accomplished. Pick the sentence starter that you like and write a paragraph about anything you want. This is a chance for you to be creative and to write something for yourself. Use the space below and a separate sheet if necessary.

If you are better with pictures, feel free to draw a picture.

Sentence Starters

One thing that make me very angry is...

Sometimes when I'm angry, I...

I need to _____ when I get angry because...

When I am angry, I feel...

_____

_____

_____

_____

_____

_____

_____

_____

Learning More About Anger

Parents/Guardians

It would be helpful if you could review and comment on the work that your child has done in this workbook. We encourage students to work with their parents on certain sections and we thank you for your cooperation. We hope that your child has had a chance to examine their behavior and to plan positively for the future. This unit has exposed students to a lot of information which we hope could be reviewed at home. We greatly appreciate your partnership in this project.

Comments: _____

_____

_____

_____

_____

_____

_____

Please feel free to contact the student's advisor or the person who assigned this workbook if you have any other questions or concerns.

Students

Now that you have completed the workbook, we urge you to provide some comments. Please comment on anything positive, e.g. "What did you like about it?" Also comment on what you did not like. If you have any suggestions, we would also like to hear them. **Congratulations for all your hard work!**

Comments: _____

_____

_____

_____

_____

_____

9 781630 268060